asian
noodles

Versatile and easy to prepare, noodles are a great stand-by.
This book contains a selection of over 40 delicious noodle dishes
that are easy to prepare at home.

PERIPLUS

ASIAN NOODLE GUIDE

The wide range of noodles and Asian ingredients available in the supermarket is a good indication of their ever-growing popularity. Versatile and easy to prepare, noodles are a great stand-by, often requiring only a few minutes soaking before they're ready.

CELLOPHANE NOODLES

Also known as bean thread vermicelli, mung bean vermicelli or glass noodles, these thin, opaque threads are made from a mixture of mung bean and tapioca starch. They have a gelatinous texture and absorb flavours well so are ideal for soups and braised dishes. Cellophane noodles need to be soaked in boiling water for 3–4 minutes before use or can be deep-fried straight from the pack.

DRIED RICE NOODLE STICKS

These translucent, flat noodles are broader and thicker than rice vermicelli and need to be soaked in warm water for 15–20 minutes before use. Because they retain an *al dente* texture during cooking, they are perfect for dishes such as Phad Thai. For a softer, more slippery texture, cook in boiling water for 3–5 minutes instead.

DRIED RICE VERMICELLI

One of Asia's most popular and versatile noodles, rice vermicelli are made from rice flour paste. They need to be soaked in boiling water for 6–7 minutes before use in stir-fries or soups. When deep-fried, rice vermicelli will expand to approximately four times its original size and is often used as a garnish.

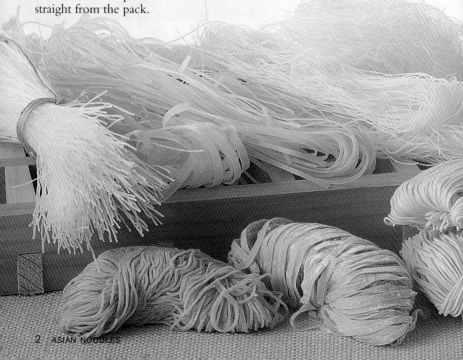

HOKKIEN NOODLES

These are thick, fresh egg noodles which have been cooked and lightly oiled before packaging. They are most often found vacuum packed and need only to be covered with boiling water for 1 minute before being drained and used in stir-fries, soups or salads.

EGG NOODLES

Made from wheat flour and eggs, these noodles are probably the most widespread in Asia and are sold in a variety of widths. Fresh egg noodles can be stored in the refrigerator for up to 1 week, then need to be plunged into boiling water for only 1 minute, while dried noodles need 3–4 minutes cooking.

FRESH RICE SHEET NOODLES

These white, flat noodles are made from rice flour and are steamed and lightly oiled before being packaged ready for use. Cover these noodles in boiling water, gently loosen and separate and drain before use. Use within a few days as they shouldn't be stored in the refrigerator—they will go hard and won't separate. They are commonly used in soups and stir-fries.

RAMEN NOODLES

These Japanese wheat flour noodles, are a popular snack all over Japan and are sold in instant form, usually with a sachet of broth. They are also available fresh and dried and need to be cooked in boiling water for 2–5 minutes.

SHANGHAI NOODLES

These thick, round egg noodles are very similar to Hokkien noodles, but have not been cooked or oiled. They are sold packaged loosely and dusted with flour. Cook in boiling water for 4–5 minutes, then rinse in cold water before use.

Clockwise from left: Cellophane noodles, Dried rice noodle sticks, Dried rice vermicelli, Hokkien, Shanghai, Ramen, Fresh rice sheet, three varieties of Egg noodles.

Soba Noodles

Are made from buckwheat or wheat flour and sometimes flavoured with green tea powder. Soba noodles are usually eaten in soups or served cold with a dipping sauce. They are available fresh and dried and need to be cooked in boiling water for about 5 minutes before use.

Somen Noodles

These fine, white Japanese noodles are made from wheat flour and are most commonly eaten cold or sometimes with a little broth. They need to be cooked in boiling water for 2 minutes before use, then rinsed in cold water and drained.

Udon Noodles

These white Japanese noodles are made from wheat flour and are sold in a variety of widths, both fresh and dried. Udon noodles should be boiled for 1–2 minutes before use and are most often eaten in soups but may also be served cold or in braised dishes.

Wheat Noodles

Available fresh or dried, these egg-free noodles are extremely versatile and need to be cooked for 2–4 minutes in boiling water, then rinsed in cold water. Fresh noodles will keep refrigerated for up to 1 week.

Clockwise from left: three varieties of Soba noodles, Somen noodles (standing and lying down), Udon noodles, Somen noodles, and Wheat noodles.

ASIAN PANTRY GUIDE

BLACK BEANS are fermented and heavily salted black soy beans. Rinse thoroughly before use. Available canned or in packets and, once opened, store in an airtight container in the refrigerator.

BLACK FUNGUS (*Cloud ear or Wood fungus*) has little flavour of its own, but is crunchy in texture. It is most commonly available dried, so must be soaked in warm water for 20 minutes.

BOK CHOY

Also known as Chinese chard or Chinese white cabbage, bok choy has fleshy white stems and green flat leaves with a mustardy taste. Both the leaves and stems are used in soups, stir-fries, as a vegetable or in salads.

CANDLENUTS are large, waxy nuts similar in size to macadamia nuts, but with a drier texture. Candlenuts cannot be eaten raw as they can be toxic. Candlenuts are roasted, then ground and used to thicken and enrich curries and sauces.

CHINESE BARBECUED PORK (*Char sui*) is a pork fillet which has been marinated in a mixture of soy sauce, five-spice powder and sugar, then barbecued over charcoal.

CHINESE COOKING WINE (*Shaosing*) is a fermented rice wine, which has a similar flavour to dry sherry.

DASHI GRANULES are made from dried kelp (kombu) and dried fish (bonito). Available as granules or as powder, dissolve in hot water to make this Japanese stock.

FISH SAUCE is a pungent salty sauce made by fermenting barrels of small fish in brine for several months. It is a popular Southeast Asian seasoning.

HOISIN SAUCE is a thick, sweet-spicy Chinese sauce made from soy beans, garlic, sugar and spices. It is used in cooking and as a dip. Once opened, store in an airtight container in the refrigerator.

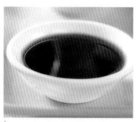

JAPANESE SOY SAUCE (*Shoyu*) is a much lighter and sweeter form than the Chinese version.

KAFFIR LIME LEAVES are shiny, dark-green leaves which release a superb fragrance in dishes. Available fresh and dried, each leaf is shaped in a figure of eight—in our recipes,

half of the figure of eight represents one leaf. Freeze any unused fresh leaves to prevent spoiling. Regular lime leaves cannot be used instead.

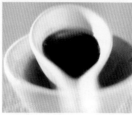

KECAP MANIS is also known as sweet soy sauce. It is a thick, dark, sweet soy sauce used in Indonesian and Malaysian cooking. If it's not available, simply stir in a little soft brown sugar to regular soy sauce until it dissolves.

LEMON GRASS is an aromatic herb, best used fresh. Trim the base, remove the tough outer layers and finely chop the inner white layers. The whole stem can also be used in dishes such as curry, but must be removed before serving. Often used in curry pastes and stir-fries.

MIRIN is a Japanese sweetened cooking wine made from rice. It is used to add sweetness to sauces, grills and glazes.

MISO PASTE is a paste made from fermented soy beans. It is used as a staple in Japanese soups, sauces, marinades and dips. Generally, the lighter the paste, the milder and sweeter the flavour.

MIZUNA is a Japanese green with a mild peppery flavour. Young leaves are often used in salads or as a garnish, while older leaves are used in stir-fries.

PONZU is a Japanese dipping sauce of equal parts Japanese soy sauce (shoyu) and lemon or lime juice.

RICE PAPER WRAPPERS are paper-thin, brittle rounds made from rice flour, salt and water. They are available dry in sealed packets and will keep indefinitely in this state. Soak each wrapper briefly in warm water before using.

RICE VINEGAR is a clear, pale yellow, mild and sweet-tasting vinegar made from fermented rice. It is commonly used in dressings and marinades.

SANSHO POWDER is a Japanese seasoning made from the dried and ground pod of the prickly ash. Because of its slightly hot, peppery, lemon-like flavour, it should be used sparingly. Sansho powder is only available ground from Asian food stores.

SESAME OIL is an aromatic oil made from roasted sesame seeds. It should be used sparingly as it has a very strong rich flavour.

SHIITAKE MUSHROOMS are a variety of fungus which grow on rotting wood. They are commonly used in Japanese and Chinese cooking. They are available fresh or dried—the dried variety must be soaked before use and their woody stems discarded. The soaking liquid can then be used as a stock.

TAMARIND is a tarty flavoured fibrous pod, often added to Thai curries. Available as a concentrate or in blocks of compressed pulp which must be soaked and strained before use.

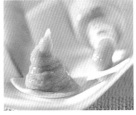

WASABI PASTE is a pungent paste made from the knobbly green root of the Japanese wasabi plant. It is often referred to as 'Japanese horseradish' because of its flavour, but is not related to horseradish. Wasabi paste is served as a condiment with sushi and noodles and is very hot—use sparingly.

ASIAN NOODLES

Asian noodles are a versatile ingredient and create great dishes from a creamy laksa to a saucy stir-fry.

CURRIED CHICKEN NOODLE SOUP

Prep time: 15 minutes
Cooking time: 1 hour
Serves 4

175 g dried thin egg noodles
2 tablespoons peanut oil
2 chicken breasts (about 250 g each)
1 onion, sliced
1 small fresh red chilli, seeded and finely chopped
1 tablespoon finely chopped fresh ginger
2 tablespoons Indian curry powder
3 cups (750 ml) chicken stock
800 ml coconut milk
300 g baby bok choy, cut into long strips
1/3 cup (20 g) fresh basil, torn

1 Cook the noodles in a large saucepan of boiling water for 3–4 minutes, or until cooked. Drain and set aside. Wipe the saucepan clean and dry.
2 Heat the oil in the dry pan and add the chicken. Cook on each side for 5 minutes, or until cooked through. Remove the chicken and keep warm.
3 Place the onion in the pan and cook over low heat for 8 minutes, or until softened but not browned. Add the chilli, ginger and curry powder and cook for a further 2 minutes. Add the chicken stock and bring to the boil. Reduce the heat and simmer for 20 minutes. Thinly slice the chicken on the diagonal.
4 Add the coconut milk to the saucepan and simmer for 10 minutes. Add the bok choy and cook for 3 minutes, then stir in the basil.
5 To serve, divide the noodles among four deep serving bowls. Top with slices of chicken and ladle in the soup. Serve immediately.

Nutrition per serve: Fat 55.5 g; Protein 42 g; Carbohydrate 43 g; Dietary fibre 7 g; Cholesterol 70.5 mg; 3470 kJ (830 cal)

Curried chicken noodle soup

NOODLE FRITTERS WITH TUNA AND GINGER SALAD

Prep time: 20 minutes
Cooking time: 30 minutes
Serves 6 (as an entrée)

70 g soba buckwheat
    noodles
1/2 cup (125 ml) milk
3 egg yolks
1 teaspoon sesame oil
2 teaspoons soy sauce
1 cup (125 g) plain flour,
    sifted
1 teaspoon baking powder
2 egg whites
3 tablespoons peanut oil
400 g tuna steaks
2 cups (40 g) mizuna leaves
2 spring onions, thinly sliced
    on the diagonal
30 g pickled ginger, julienned
1 tablespoon black sesame
    seeds
lime wedges, to garnish

Dressing
1 teaspoon wasabi paste
2 tablespoons ponzu
1 teaspoon pickled ginger
    syrup

1 Cook the noodles in a large saucepan of boiling salted water for 2–3 minutes, or until tender. Rinse under cold running water, drain and cut into 2 cm lengths.
2 Combine the milk, egg yolks, sesame oil and soy sauce. Sift the flour and baking powder into a large bowl and make a well in the centre. Stir in the milk mixture until smooth, then mix in the noodles. In a clean bowl, beat the egg whites with electric beaters until soft peaks form. Gently fold the whites into the noodle mixture.
3 Heat 1 tablespoon of the peanut oil in a non-stick frying pan over medium heat. Add 1/3 cup (80 ml) of the batter and cook on each side for 2 minutes, or until golden. Remove and keep warm. Repeat to make 6 fritters in total.
4 Preheat a chargrill pan. Brush the tuna with the remaining oil and season. Sear on both sides for 1–2 minutes, or until cooked to your liking. Combine the mizuna, spring onion and ginger in a large bowl.
5 To make the dressing, combine the wasabi, ponzu and ginger syrup. Add to the mizuna mixture and toss well. Thinly slice the tuna.
6 Place each fritter on a serving plate and top with salad mix and tuna slices. Sprinkle with the sesame seeds and garnish with a wedge of lime.

Nutrition per serve: Fat 18.5 g;
Protein 25 g; Carbohydrate 27 g;
Dietary fibre 1.5 g; Cholesterol
116.5 mg; 1555 kJ (370 cal)

Noodle fritters with tuna
and ginger salad (top), and
Pork and glass noodle soup

PORK AND GLASS NOODLE SOUP

Prep time: 10 minutes
Cooking time: 20 minutes
Serves 4

150 g cellophane noodles
2 teaspoons peanut oil
2 teaspoons grated fresh
    ginger
1.25 litres chicken stock
1/3 cup (80 ml) Chinese rice
    wine
1 tablespoon hoisin sauce
1 tablespoon soy sauce
4 spring onions, thinly sliced
    on the diagonal, plus extra,
    to garnish
300 g sliced Chinese roast
    pork

1 Soak the noodles in a large bowl with enough boiling water to cover, for 3–4 minutes. Drain.
2 Heat the oil in a large saucepan. Add the ginger and stir-fry for 1 minute. Add the stock, Chinese rice wine, hoisin and soy sauces and simmer for 10 minutes. Add the spring onion and roast pork, then cook for a further 5 minutes.
3 Divide the noodles among four large bowls. Ladle in the soup and arrange the pork on top. Garnish with extra spring onion.

Nutrition per serve: Fat 11.5 g;
Protein 26 g; Carbohydrate 38 g;
Dietary fibre 1 g; Cholesterol
67 mg; 1565 kJ (375 cal)

CRISPY DUCK WITH HOKKIEN NOODLES

Prep time: 20 minutes
Cooking time: 40 minutes
Serves 4

4 duck breasts (200 g each)
1 tablespoon five-spice powder
400 g Hokkien noodles
100 g snow peas
1 tablespoon peanut oil
2 cloves garlic, crushed
2 teaspoons finely chopped fresh ginger
1 small fresh red chilli, seeded and finely chopped
3 tablespoons soy sauce
1 tablespoon hoisin sauce
2 tablespoons plum sauce
1 tablespoon honey
50 g bean sprouts
3 spring onions, cut into thin strips
150 g cucumber, cut into thin strips

1 Preheat the oven to very hot 230°C (450°F/Gas 8). Place the duck breasts in a roasting tin, skin-side up. Combine the five-spice powder and 2 teaspoons salt and press onto each breast. Roast for 35 minutes. Rest for 5 minutes, then cut into thin slices.
2 Soak the noodles in boiling water for 1 minute. Drain and place in a bowl. Blanch the snow peas for 15 seconds.
3 Heat the peanut oil in a saucepan and cook the garlic, ginger and chilli for 30 seconds. Combine the soy, hoisin and plum sauces, honey and 2 tablespoons water, add to the pan and cook for 1 minute.
4 Combine the duck, noodles, snow peas, bean sprouts, spring onion, cucumber and the warm sauce and serve.

Nutrition per serve: Fat 17.5 g; Protein 48 g; Carbohydrate 71 g; Dietary fibre 5 g; Cholesterol 233 mg; 2640 kJ (630 cal)

SPRING ROLLS

Prep time: 50 minutes
Cooking time: 30 minutes
Makes 40

50 g cellophane noodles
1 tablespoon oil
2 large cloves garlic, crushed
6 spring onions, finely chopped
3 teaspoons finely chopped fresh ginger
400 g chicken mince
1 tablespoon finely chopped fresh coriander root
2 tablespoons finely chopped fresh coriander leaves
1 tablespoon finely chopped fresh Vietnamese mint
1 carrot (125 g), grated
1 tablespoon fish sauce
2 tablespoons sweet chilli sauce
3 tablespoons soy sauce
40 small spring roll wrappers
oil, extra, for deep-frying
sweet chilli sauce, to serve

1 Soak the noodles in boiling water for 3–4 minutes. Drain and cut into 4 cm lengths.
2 Heat the oil in a large saucepan. Cook the garlic, spring onion and ginger over medium heat for 1–2 minutes, or until soft. Add the mince and cook, breaking up any lumps, for 3–4 minutes, or until just cooked. Stir in the noodles, coriander root and leaves, mint and carrot and cook for 1 minute. Add the fish, sweet chilli and soy sauces and cook for 2 minutes, or until the mixture is dry. Cool.
3 Place 1 tablespoon of the mixture in the centre of a wrapper. Brush the edge with water and roll up, tucking in the ends as you go. Cover with a clean tea towel.
4 Fill a deep heavy-based saucepan one third full of oil. Heat to 190°C (375°F), or until a cube of bread browns in 10 seconds. Cook the spring rolls in batches for 30–60 seconds, or until golden brown. Drain. Serve with sweet chilli sauce.

Nutrition per roll: Fat 1.7 g; Protein 2.5 g; Carbohydrate 6 g; Dietary fibre 0.5 g; Cholesterol 9 mg; 200 kJ (50 cal)

Crispy duck with Hokkien noodles (top), and Spring rolls

CRAB AND CORN EGGFLOWER NOODLE BROTH

Prep time: 15 minutes
Cooking time: 15 minutes
Serves 4

75 g dried thin egg noodles
1 tablespoon peanut oil
1 teaspoon finely chopped fresh ginger
3 spring onions, thinly sliced, white and green parts separated
1.25 litres chicken stock
1/3 cup (80 ml) mirin
250 g baby corn, sliced on the diagonal into 1 cm slices
175 g fresh crab meat
1 tablespoon cornflour mixed with 1 tablespoon water
2 eggs, lightly beaten
2 teaspoons lime juice
1 tablespoon soy sauce
1/4 cup (7 g) torn fresh coriander leaves

1 Cook the noodles in boiling salted water for 3 minutes, or until just tender. Drain and rinse under cold water.
2 Heat the oil in a large heavy-based saucepan. Add the ginger and the spring onion (white part) and cook over medium heat for 1–2 minutes. Add the stock, mirin and corn and bring to the boil. Simmer for 5 minutes. Stir in the noodles, crab meat and cornflour mixture. Return to a simmer, stirring constantly until it thickens. Reduce the heat and pour in the egg in a thin stream, stirring constantly—do not boil. Gently stir in the lime juice, soy sauce and half the coriander.
3 Divide the noodles among four bowls and ladle the soup on top. Garnish with the spring onion (green part) and coriander leaves.

Nutrition per serve: Fat 9 g; Protein 18 g; Carbohydrate 31 g; Dietary fibre 2.5 g; Cholesterol 130 mg; 1160 kJ (275 cal)

CHICKEN AND NOODLE SALAD WITH CASHEWS

Prep time: 20 minutes +
    2 hours marinating
Cooking time: 20 minutes
Serves 4

2 cloves garlic, peeled
1/4 cup (60 ml) fish sauce
1/4 cup (60 ml) lime juice
2 teaspoons chilli paste
2 tablespoons soft brown sugar
2 cups (60 g) firmly packed fresh coriander leaves
1 cup (155 g) unsalted roasted cashews, chopped
3 tablespoons vegetable oil
650 g chicken thigh fillets or breast fillets
375 g rice noodle sticks
200 g tomatoes, diced
1/4 cup (7 g) fresh coriander leaves, extra

1 Combine the garlic, fish sauce, lime juice, chilli paste, brown sugar, coriander and half the cashews in a food processor until smooth. With the motor running, slowly add the oil and blend until combined.
2 Place the chicken in a bowl with 1/2 cup (125 ml) of the dressing. Cover and marinate in the refrigerator for at least 2 hours.
3 Heat a grill or non-stick frying pan. Add the chicken. Cook on each side for 5–6 minutes, or until cooked through. Rest for 5 minutes, then cut into thin strips.
4 Cook the noodles in a saucepan of boiling water for 3-5 minutes, or until just tender. Rinse and drain. Toss with the tomato and the remaining dressing.
5 Place the noodles on a large serving platter or on individual plates. Top with the chicken, the remaining cashews and extra coriander leaves. Serve warm.

Nutrition per serve: Fat 42.5 g; Protein 48 g; Carbohydrate 80 g; Dietary fibre 4.5 g; Cholesterol 112 mg; 3750 kJ (895 cal)

Crab and corn eggflower noodle broth (top), and Chicken and noodle salad with cashews

PORK AND NOODLE BALLS WITH SWEET CHILLI SAUCE

Prep time: 30 minutes
Cooking time: 20 minutes
Makes 30

Dipping sauce
1/3 cup (80 ml) sweet chilli sauce
2 teaspoons mirin
2 teaspoons finely chopped fresh ginger
1/2 cup (125 ml) Japanese soy sauce

250 g Hokkien noodles
300 g pork mince
6 spring onions, finely chopped
2 cloves garlic, crushed
1/3 cup (20 g) finely chopped fresh coriander leaves
1 tablespoon fish sauce
2 tablespoons oyster sauce
11/2 tablespoons lime juice
peanut oil, for deep-frying

1 To make the dipping sauce, place the sweet chilli sauce, mirin, ginger and Japanese soy sauce in a bowl and stir until combined.
2 Place the noodles in a bowl and cover with boiling water. Soak for 1 minute, or until tender. Drain very well and pat dry with paper towels. Cut the noodles into 5 cm lengths, then transfer to a large bowl. Add the pork mince, spring onion, garlic, coriander leaves, fish sauce, oyster sauce and lime juice and combine the mixture well using your hands, making sure the pork is evenly distributed throughout the noodles.
3 Using a tablespoon of mixture at a time, roll each spoonful into a ball to make 30 in total, shaping and pressing each ball firmly with your hands to ensure they stick together during cooking.
4 Fill a wok or large saucepan one third full of oil and heat to warm 170°C (325°F), or until a cube of bread browns in 20 seconds. Deep-fry the pork balls in batches for 2–3 minutes, or until golden and cooked through. Drain on paper towels. Serve hot with the dipping sauce.

Nutrition per ball: Fat 2 g; Protein 3 g; Carbohydrate 5.5 g; Dietary fibre 0.5 g; Cholesterol 7 mg; 230 kJ (55 cal)

Note: These pork and noodle balls can be made in advance and frozen in an airtight container for up to 3 months, then reheated in the oven just before serving. Allow them to defrost in the refrigerator, then place in a moderately hot 200°C (400°F/Gas 6) oven for 10 minutes, or until crisp and heated through.

Storage: The dipping sauce can be stored in an airtight jar in the refrigerator for 1 week. It is best made in advance to allow the flavours to infuse.

Variation: Serve the Pork and Noodle Balls with a peanut satay sauce. Place 1 cup (160 g) unsalted roasted peanuts in a food processor and process until finely chopped. Heat 2 tablespoons oil in a saucepan. Add 1 chopped onion and cook over medium heat for 5 minutes, or until softened. Add 2 crushed cloves garlic, 2 teaspoons finely chopped fresh ginger, 1/2 teaspoon chilli powder and 1 teaspoon ground cumin, and cook, stirring, for 2 minutes. Add 12/3 cups (410 ml) coconut milk, 3 tablespoons soft brown sugar and the chopped peanuts. Reduce the heat and cook for 5 minutes, or until the sauce thickens. Add 1 tablespoon lemon juice and season to taste. (If you prefer a smoother sauce, blend the sauce ingredients in a food processor for 30 seconds.)

Pork and noodle balls with sweet chilli sauce

STEAMED PRAWN RICE NOODLE ROLLS

Prep time: 20 minutes +
15 minutes soaking
Cooking time: 5 minutes
Makes 12

Dipping sauce
2 tablespoons light soy sauce
3 tablespoons rice vinegar

3 dried shiitake mushrooms
350 g raw prawns, peeled and deveined
4 spring onions, chopped
60 g snow peas, chopped
2 teaspoons finely chopped fresh ginger
2 cloves garlic, crushed
1/2 cup (15 g) chopped fresh coriander leaves
100 g water chestnuts, chopped
1 teaspoon sesame oil
1 tablespoon light soy sauce
1 egg white
1 teaspoon cornflour
300 g fresh rice sheet noodles

1 To make the dipping sauce, combine the soy sauce and rice vinegar.
2 Cover the mushrooms with hot water and soak for 15 minutes. Drain, discard the stalks, and finely chop the caps.
3 Mince the prawns in a food processor. Add the mushrooms, spring onion, snow peas, ginger, garlic, coriander, water chestnuts, sesame oil, soy sauce and a pinch of salt. Add the egg white and cornflour and pulse until smooth.
4 Line a large bamboo steamer with baking paper and place over a wok of simmering water (ensure the base doesn't touch the water). Gently unfold the rice sheet noodle and cut into six 15 cm squares. Spread 1/4 cup (60 ml) filling evenly over each square and roll firmly to form a log. Steam, covered, in a wok for 5 minutes. Cut each roll in half and serve with the sauce.

Nutrition per roll: Fat 1 g; Protein 8 g; Carbohydrate 12 g; Dietary fibre 1 g; Cholesterol 43.5 mg; 375 kJ (90 cal)

TOFU AND ASIAN MUSHROOM NOODLE SOUP

Prep time: 20 minutes
Cooking time: 15 minutes
Serves 4

2 dried Chinese mushrooms
10 g dried black fungus
1 tablespoon vegetable oil
6 spring onions, thickly sliced on the diagonal
1 fresh red chilli, seeded and chopped
60 g oyster mushrooms, sliced
60 g Swiss brown mushrooms, sliced
11/2 tablespoons dashi granules
3 tablespoons light soy sauce
11/2 tablespoons mirin
125 g dried wheat noodles
200 g water spinach, cut into 4 cm slices
300 g firm tofu, cut into 2 cm cubes
1/3 cup (10 g) fresh whole coriander leaves

1 Soak the Chinese mushrooms in 1 cup (250 ml) hot water. Squeeze dry and reserve the liquid. Discard the stalks and finely chop the caps. Cover the black fungus in hot water and soak until soft. Drain.
2 Heat the oil in a large saucepan or wok. Cook the Chinese mushrooms, black fungus, spring onion and chilli over high heat for 1 minute. Add the oyster and Swiss brown mushrooms and cook for 2 minutes.
3 Stir in the dashi, soy sauce, mirin, reserved mushroom liquid and 1.5 litres water. Bring to the boil, then stir in the noodles. Cook over medium heat for 5 minutes, or until soft.
4 Add the water spinach and cook for 2 minutes, then add the tofu and coriander. Serve at once.

Nutrition per serve: Fat 10.5 g; Protein 17 g; Carbohydrate 26 g; Dietary fibre 5.5 g; Cholesterol 0 mg; 1105 kJ (265 cal)

Steamed prawn rice noodle rolls (top), and Tofu and Asian mushroom noodle soup

SINGAPORE NOODLES

Prep time: 20 minutes
Cooking time: 10 minutes
Serves 4

375 g thin fresh egg noodles
10 g dried Chinese mushrooms
2 1/2 teaspoons sugar
1 1/2 tablespoons soy sauce
2 tablespoons Chinese rice wine
1 1/2 tablespoons Indian madras curry powder
150 ml coconut milk
1/2 cup (125 ml) chicken stock
2 eggs
1 tablespoon sesame oil
3 tablespoons vegetable oil
2 cloves garlic, finely chopped
1 tablespoon finely chopped fresh ginger
2 small fresh red chillies, seeded and finely chopped
3 spring onions, sliced
300 g small raw prawns, peeled, deveined and halved
150 g Chinese roast pork, thinly sliced
120 g frozen peas
fresh coriander, to garnish

1 Cook the noodles in boiling salted water for 1 minute. Drain and rinse in cold water.
2 Soak the mushrooms in a bowl with 1/2 cup (125 ml) hot water for 10 minutes. Drain and reserve the liquid, then discard the hard stalks and finely slice the caps. Combine the reserved liquid with the sugar, soy sauce, rice wine, curry powder, coconut milk and stock.
3 Lightly beat the eggs and sesame oil together.
4 Heat a wok and add 2 tablespoons of the oil. Cook the garlic, ginger, chilli and mushrooms for 30 seconds. Add the spring onion, prawns, pork, peas and noodles. Stir in the mushroom liquid mixture. Add the egg mixture in a thin stream and toss until warmed through. Serve in deep bowls, garnished with coriander leaves.

Nutrition per serve: Fat 34.5 g; Protein 43 g; Carbohydrate 58 g; Dietary fibre 5.5 g; Cholesterol 251 mg; 3010 kJ (720 cal)

UDON NOODLE STIR-FRY WITH MISO DRESSING

Prep time: 15 minutes
Cooking time: 10 minutes
Serves 4

1 tablespoon white miso
1 tablespoon Japanese soy sauce
2 tablespoons sake
1/2 teaspoon sugar
400 g fresh udon noodles
1 tablespoon peanut oil
5 spring onions, cut into 5 cm lengths
1 red capsicum, thinly sliced
100 g fresh shiitake mushrooms, sliced
150 g snow peas, sliced lengthways into strips

1 Combine the miso with the soy sauce to form a smooth paste. Add the sake and sugar and mix well.
2 Cook the noodles in a large saucepan of salted boiling water for 1–2 minutes, or until tender and plump. Drain and rinse under cold water.
3 Heat the oil in a wok or large frying pan over high heat and swirl to coat. Add the spring onion and capsicum and toss frequently for 1–2 minutes, or until softened slightly. Add the mushrooms and snow peas and stir-fry for 2–3 minutes, or until tender.
4 Add the noodles and miso mixture to the wok and toss until well combined. Serve immediately.

Nutrition per serve: Fat 5.5 g; Protein 8 g; Carbohydrate 34 g; Dietary fibre 4 g; Cholesterol 0 mg; 925 kJ (220 cal)

Note: If fresh shiitake mushrooms are not available, use Swiss brown or oyster mushrooms instead.

Singapore noodles (top), and Udon noodle stir-fry with miso dressing

NOODLE AND CRAB CAKE WITH BLACK BEAN SAUCE

Prep time: 25 minutes
Cooking time: 20 minutes
Serves 4

125 g thin egg noodles
3 tablespoons black bean sauce
1/2 cup (125 ml) chicken stock
1 teaspoon cornflour
2 tablespoons peanut oil
2 cloves garlic, crushed
1 tablespoon finely chopped fresh ginger
4 spring onions, cut on the diagonal
1 small carrot, julienned
1/2 red capsicum, julienned
2 x 170 g cans white crab meat
1 cup (90 g) bean sprouts
10 eggs
1/2 cup (15 g) firmly packed fresh coriander leaves
fresh coriander leaves, extra, to garnish

1 Cook the noodles in a saucepan of boiling water for 1 minute, or until separate and tender. Drain and rinse under cold water.

2 Place the black bean sauce and chicken stock in a saucepan and cook over medium heat for 6–8 minutes, or until reduced by half. Combine the cornflour

Crab and noodle cake with black bean sauce

and 1 tablespoon water, then add to the sauce, stirring, until it thickens. Set aside.

3 Heat 1 tablespoon of the peanut oil in a frying pan. Add the garlic and ginger and cook over medium heat for 30 seconds. Add the spring onion, carrot and capsicum and cook for 2–3 minutes. Remove from the heat and mix in the crab meat, bean sprouts and noodles.

4 Beat the eggs together in a bowl and season lightly with salt and freshly ground black pepper. Add the vegetable and crab mixture, then stir in the coriander.

5 Heat the remaining oil in a deep-sided 23 cm non-stick frying pan. Add the egg and vegetable mixture, then reduce the heat to very low and cook, covered, for 10 minutes, or until it is firm and starting to come away from the side of the pan—check occasionally to make sure it doesn't stick to the base of the pan.

6 Place under a hot grill to cook the top—the finished dish should be quite firm. Turn the cake out onto a large serving plate and cut into wedges.

7 Reheat the black bean sauce in a small saucepan over low heat and place

in a serving bowl. Spoon the sauce over warm wedges of the cake and garnish with fresh coriander leaves.

Nutrition per serve: Fat 22.5 g; Protein 31 g; Carbohydrate 24 g; Dietary fibre 3 g; Cholesterol 517.5 mg; 1760 kJ (420 cal)

Note: If you prefer, you can use fresh crab meat instead of canned. Make sure you squeeze out any excess moisture and remove any bits of shell or cartilage.

CRAB AND SPINACH SOBA NOODLE SALAD

Prep time: 15 minutes
Cooking time: 5 minutes
Serves 4

1/4 cup (60 ml) Japanese
  rice vinegar
1/2 cup (125 ml) mirin
2 tablespoons soy sauce
1 teaspoon finely chopped
  fresh ginger
400 g English spinach
250 g fresh cooked
  crab meat
250 g soba noodles
2 teaspoons sesame oil
2 spring onions, finely
  chopped
1 sheet nori, cut into
  matchstick-size strips

1 Combine the rice vinegar, mirin, soy sauce and ginger in a small bowl. Set aside.
2 Bring a large saucepan of salted water to the boil. Blanch the spinach for 15–20 seconds, then remove with a slotted spoon (reserve the water in the pan). Place the spinach in a bowl of ice-cold water for 30 seconds. Drain and squeeze out the moisture, then coarsely chop. Combine with the crab meat and 2 tablespoons of the rice vinegar mixture.
3 Bring the pan of water back to the boil and cook the noodles for 5 minutes, or until just tender. Drain, then rinse under cold water. Toss with the sesame oil, spring onion and the remaining dressing. Divide the noodles among individual bowls, top with the spinach and crab meat and scatter with nori.

Nutrition per serve: Fat 3.5 g; Protein 20 g; Carbohydrate 49 g; Dietary fibre 4.5 g; Cholesterol 52.5 mg; 1245 kJ (295 cal)

LAMB WITH HOKKIEN NOODLES AND SOUR SAUCE

Prep time: 25 minutes
Cooking time: 15 minutes
Serves 4–6

450 g Hokkien noodles
2 tablespoons vegetable oil
375 g lamb backstrap,
  thinly sliced against
  the grain
75 g red Asian shallots,
  peeled and thinly sliced
3 cloves garlic, crushed
2 teaspoons finely chopped
  fresh ginger
1 small fresh red chilli,
  seeded and finely chopped
11/2 tablespoons red curry
  paste
125 g snow peas, trimmed
  and cut in half on the
  diagonal
1 small carrot, julienned
1/2 cup (125 ml) chicken
  stock
15 g palm sugar, grated
1 tablespoon lime juice
small whole basil leaves,
  to garnish

1 Cover the noodles with boiling water and soak for 1 minute. Drain and set aside.
2 Heat 1 tablespoon of the oil in a wok and swirl to coat. Stir-fry the lamb in batches over high heat for 2–3 minutes, or until it just changes colour. Remove to a side plate.
3 Add the remaining oil, then the shallots, garlic, ginger and chilli and stir-fry for 1–2 minutes. Stir in the curry paste and cook for 1 minute. Add the snow peas, carrot and the lamb and combine. Cook over high heat, tossing often, for 1–2 minutes.
4 Add the stock, palm sugar and lime juice, toss to combine and cook for 2–3 minutes. Add the noodles and cook for 1 minute, or until heated through. Divide among serving bowls and garnish with the basil.

Nutrition per serve (6): Fat 11 g; Protein 22 g; Carbohydrate 44 g; Dietary fibre 3 g; Cholesterol 51 mg; 1540 kJ (365 cal)

Crab and spinach soba noodle salad (top), and Lamb with Hokkien noodles and sour sauce

CHICKEN AND PUMPKIN LAKSA

Prep time: 10 minutes +
  20 minutes soaking
Cooking time: 35 minutes
Serves 4

Paste
2 birds eye chillies, seeded
  and roughly chopped
2 stems lemon grass, white
  part only, roughly chopped
4 red Asian shallots, peeled
1 tablespoon roughly
  chopped fresh ginger
1 teaspoon ground turmeric
3 candlenuts, optional

110 g dried rice noodle
  sticks
1 tablespoon peanut oil
250 g butternut pumpkin,
  cut into 2 cm chunks
800 ml coconut milk
600 g chicken breast fillets,
  cut into cubes
2 tablespoons lime juice
1 tablespoon fish sauce
1 cup (90 g) bean sprouts
1/2 cup (15 g) torn fresh basil
1/2 cup (10 g) torn fresh mint
1/2 cup (50 g) unsalted
  peanuts, toasted and
  chopped
1 lime, cut into quarters

1 Place all the paste
ingredients in a food
processor with
1 tablespoon water and
blend until smooth.

Chicken and pumpkin
laksa (top), and Buckwheat
noodles with sweet and
sour capsicum

2 Soak the noodles in
boiling water for
15–20 minutes. Drain.
3 Heat the oil in a wok
and swirl to coat. Add
the paste and stir over
low heat for 5 minutes,
or until aromatic. Add
the pumpkin and
coconut milk and
simmer for 10 minutes.
Add the chicken and
simmer for 20 minutes.
Stir in the lime juice and
fish sauce.
4 Divide the noodles
among four deep bowls,
then ladle on the soup.
Garnish with the bean
sprouts, basil, mint,
peanuts and lime.

Nutrition per serve: Fat 60 g;
Protein 43 g; Carbohydrate 34 g;
Dietary fibre 7 g; Cholesterol
103.5 mg; 3505 kJ (835 cal)

BUCKWHEAT NOODLES WITH SWEET AND SOUR CAPSICUM

Prep time: 20 minutes
Cooking time: 15 minutes
Serves 4

3 capsicums (preferably red,
  green and yellow)
2 tablespoons vegetable oil
5 teaspoons sesame oil
2 star anise
1/4 cup (60 ml) red wine
  vinegar
1 tablespoon fish sauce
1/2 cup (125 g) sugar
300 g buckwheat noodles

1/2 tablespoon balsamic
  vinegar
1/2 teaspoon sugar, extra
2 spring onions, finely sliced
2 tablespoons sesame
  seeds, lightly toasted

1 Thinly slice the
capsicums. Heat the oil
and 1 teaspoon sesame
oil in a saucepan over
medium heat cook the
star anise for 1 minute,
or until the oil begins
to smoke. Add the
capsicum and stir for
2 minutes. Reduce the
heat to low and cook,
covered, for 5 minutes,
stirring occasionally.
Increase to medium heat
and add the vinegar, fish
sauce and sugar, stirring
until dissolved. Boil for
2 minutes, then remove
from the heat and cool.
Remove the star anise.
Drain and place the
capsicum in a bowl.
2 Cook the noodles in
a saucepan of boiling
water for 5 minutes.
Drain and rinse.
3 Combine the balsamic
vinegar, remaining
sesame oil, extra sugar
and 1/2 teaspoon salt,
stirring until the sugar
dissolves. Add the
noodles and toss to coat,
then combine with the
capsicum and spring
onion. Sprinkle with the
sesame seeds and serve.

Nutrition per serve: Fat 17.5 g;
Protein 13 g; Carbohydrate 91 g;
Dietary fibre 2 g; Cholesterol
0 mg; 2280 kJ (545 cal)

BEEF PHO

Prep time: 15 minutes +
15 minutes soaking
Cooking time: 35 minutes
Serves 4

200 g rice noodle sticks
1.5 litres beef stock
1 star anise
4 cm piece fresh ginger,
sliced
2 pigs trotters (ask your
butcher to cut in half)
1/2 onion, studded with
2 cloves
2 stems lemon grass,
pounded
2 cloves garlic, pounded
1/4 teaspoon white pepper
1 tablespoon fish sauce
400 g beef fillet, partially
frozen, sliced thinly
1 cup (90 g) bean sprouts
2 spring onions, thinly sliced
on the diagonal
1/2 cup (25 g) fresh
coriander leaves, chopped
1/2 cup (25 g) fresh
Vietnamese mint, chopped
1 fresh red chilli, thinly sliced
fresh red chillies, extra,
to serve
fresh Vietnamese mint, extra,
to serve
fresh coriander leaves, extra,
to serve
2 limes, cut into quarters
fish sauce, extra, to serve

1 Soak the noodles in
boiling water for
15–20 minutes. Drain.
2 Bring the stock, star
anise, ginger, trotters,
onion, lemon grass,
garlic and white pepper
to the boil in a large
saucepan. Reduce the
heat and simmer for
30 minutes. Strain,
return to the pan and
stir in the fish sauce.
3 Divide the noodles
among bowls, then top
with beef strips, sprouts,
spring onion, coriander,
mint and chilli. Ladle on
the broth.
4 Place the extra chilli,
mint, coriander, lime
quarters and fish sauce
in small bowls on a
platter, serve with the
soup and allow your
guests to help themselves.

Nutrition per serve: Fat 12 g;
Protein 43 g; Carbohydrate 37 g;
Dietary fibre 3 g; Cholesterol
98.5 mg; 1780 kJ (425 cal)

RAMEN NOODLE SOUP WITH ROAST PORK AND GREENS

Prep time: 15 minutes
Cooking time: 10 minutes
Serves 4

15 g dried shiitake
mushrooms
350 g Chinese broccoli,
trimmed and cut into
4 cm lengths
375 g fresh ramen noodles
1.5 litres chicken stock
3 tablespoons soy sauce
1 teaspoon sugar
350 g Chinese roast pork,
thinly sliced
1 small fresh red chilli,
seeded and thinly sliced

1 Soak the mushrooms
in 1/2 cup (125 ml) hot
water until softened.
Squeeze the mushrooms
dry, reserving the liquid.
Discard the hard stalks,
then finely slice the caps.
2 Blanch the broccoli
in a large saucepan of
boiling salted water for
3 minutes, or until
tender but firm to the
bite. Drain, then refresh
in cold water.
3 Cook the noodles in a
large saucepan of boiling
water for 3 minutes, or
until just softened.
Drain, rinse under cold
water, then set aside.
4 Place the stock in a
large saucepan and bring
to the boil. Add the
sliced mushrooms and
reserved mushroom
liquid, soy sauce and
sugar. Simmer for
2 minutes, then add
the broccoli.
5 Divide the noodles
among four large bowls.
Ladle on the hot stock
and vegetables. Top
with the pork and sliced
chilli. Serve hot.

Nutrition per serve: Fat 6 g;
Protein 37 g; Carbohydrate 28 g;
Dietary fibre 5 g; Cholesterol
78 mg; 1330 kJ (320 cal)

Beef pho (top), and Ramen
noodle soup with roast
pork and greens

SESAME-CRUSTED EGGPLANT AND NOODLE STACK WITH DUCK

Prep time: 30 minutes +
  30 minutes standing
Cooking time: 20 minutes
Serves 4

1 eggplant
1 Chinese roast duck
1 egg, lightly beaten
1 teaspoon fish sauce
1 cup (155 g) sesame seeds
vegetable oil, for deep-frying
500 g fresh rice noodles
  (0.5 cm thick strips)
3 tablespoons finely sliced
  spring onion
1/2 teaspoon sesame oil
1 1/2 tablespoons vegetable
  oil, extra
1 small fresh red chilli,
  seeded and finely
  chopped
2 tablespoons finely
  chopped garlic
1 tablespoon finely sliced
  fresh ginger
1 red capsicum, cut into
  1 cm cubes
12 fresh basil leaves,
  roughly torn into strips
2 1/2 tablespoons hoisin
  sauce
2 teaspoons light soy sauce
1 tablespoon rice wine

1 Cut the eggplant into eight 0.5 cm thick rounds, then place in a colander over a plate. Sprinkle with salt, toss

Sesame-crusted eggplant and noodle stack with duck

to coat and set aside for at least 30 minutes. Remove the skin and the flesh from the duck. Roughly chop the flesh into 1 cm x 3 cm lengths. Rinse the eggplant and pat dry with paper towels. Whisk together the egg and fish sauce in a bowl. Dip each slice of eggplant in egg then in sesame seeds. Lay each slice on a tray lined with baking paper—place a sheet of baking paper between each layer too.

2 Fill a large heavy-based saucepan or deep-fryer one third full of vegetable oil and heat to 170°C (325°F), or until a cube of bread browns in 20 seconds. Cook the eggplant until golden brown on both sides. Drain on paper towels and keep warm.

3 In a bowl, combine the rice noodles with the spring onion, sesame oil and 1/2 teaspoon vegetable oil. Toss to coat the noodles well, then divide into eight equal portions. Heat a large non-stick frying pan over medium-high heat. Place greased egg rings in the pan and fill each with one portion of rice noodles. Press down firmly and cook for 2–3 minutes each side, or until lightly browned. Remove and keep warm.

4 Heat a wok over medium high heat and add the remaining vegetable oil. When hot, add the chilli, garlic and ginger and cook for 1–2 minutes. Add the capsicum and cook for a further 2 minutes, then add the duck. Toss well and stir in the hoisin sauce, soy sauce and rice wine. Toss until combined and until the sauce thickens slightly. Remove from the heat.

5 To serve, place a noodle pancake on a plate, spoon on some of the duck and capsicum mixture, then top with a slice of the sesame-crusted eggplant. Serve immediately. This stack is great with a crisp green salad of Asian salad greens such as mizuna or tatsoi.

Nutrition per stack: Fat 24 g; Protein 15 g; Carbohydrate 16 g; Dietary fibre 4 g; Cholesterol 68 mg; 1416 kJ (340 cal)

FIVE-SPICE DUCK AND SOMEN NOODLE SOUP

Prep time: 10 minutes
Cooking time: 30 minutes
Serves 4

4 duck breasts, skin on
1 teaspoon five-spice powder
1 teaspoon peanut oil
200 g dried somen noodles

Star anise broth
1 litre chicken stock
3 whole star anise
5 spring onions, chopped
1/4 cup (5 g) chopped fresh coriander leaves

1 Preheat the oven to moderately hot 200°C (400°F/Gas 6). Trim the duck breast of excess fat, then lightly sprinkle both sides with the five-spice powder.
2 Heat the oil in a large frying pan. Add the duck skin-side down and cook over medium heat for 2–3 minutes, or until brown and crisp. Turn and cook the other side for 3 minutes. Transfer to a baking tray and cook, skin-side up, for another 8–10 minutes, or until cooked to your liking.
3 Meanwhile, place the chicken stock and star anise in a small saucepan. Bring to the boil, then reduce the heat and simmer for 5 minutes.

Add the spring onion and coriander and simmer for 5 minutes.
4 Cook the noodles in a saucepan of boiling water for 2 minutes, or until soft. Drain and divide among four bowls. Ladle the broth on the noodles and top each bowl with one sliced duck breast.

Nutrition per serve: Fat 9.5 g; Protein 31 g; Carbohydrate 38 g; Dietary fibre 2.5 g; Cholesterol 138.5 mg; 1510 kJ (360 cal)

TERIYAKI BEEF WITH GREENS AND CRISPY NOODLES

Prep time: 20 minutes +
  2 hours marinating
Cooking time: 15 minutes
Serves 4

450 g sirloin steak, cut into thin strips
100 ml teriyaki marinade
vegetable oil, for deep-frying
100 g dried rice vermicelli
2 tablespoons peanut oil
1 onion, sliced
3 cloves garlic, crushed
1 fresh red chilli, seeded and finely chopped
200 g carrots, julienned
600 g choy sum, cut into 3 cm lengths
1 tablespoon lime juice

1 Combine the beef and teriyaki marinade in a non-metallic bowl and marinate for 2 hours.

2 Fill a wok one third full of oil and heat to 190°C (375°F), or until a cube of bread browns in 10 seconds. Separate the noodles into small bundles and deep-fry until they sizzle and puff up. Drain well on paper towels. Drain the oil, and carefully pour into a heatproof bowl to cool before discarding.
3 Heat 1 tablespoon of the peanut oil in the wok. When the oil is nearly smoking, add the beef (reserving the marinade) and cook in batches over high heat for 1–2 minutes. Remove to a plate. Heat the remaining oil. Add the onion and stir-fry for 3–4 minutes. Add the garlic and chilli and cook for 30 seconds. Add the carrot and choy sum and stir-fry for 3–4 minutes, or until tender.
4 Return the beef to the wok with the lime juice and reserved marinade and cook over high heat for 3 minutes. Add the noodles, toss well briefly, and serve immediately.

Nutrition per serve: Fat 20 g; Protein 35 g; Carbohydrate 23 g; Dietary fibre 4.5 g; Cholesterol 86.5 mg; 1720 kJ (410 cal)

Five-spice duck and somen noodle soup (top), and Teriyaki beef with greens and crispy noodles

ORANGE SWEET POTATO AND FRIED NOODLE SALAD

Prep time: 20 minutes
Cooking time: 35 minutes
Serves 4–6

1.25 kg orange sweet potato, peeled and cut into 2 cm chunks
2 tablespoons light oil
200 g roasted unsalted cashews
1 cup (50 g) finely chopped fresh coriander leaves
100 g packet fried noodles

Dressing
3/4 teaspoon red curry paste
90 ml coconut milk
2 tablespoons lime juice
11/2 tablespoons soft brown sugar
2 tablespoons light oil
4 cloves garlic, finely chopped
1 tablespoon finely chopped fresh ginger

1 Preheat the oven to moderately hot 200°C (400°F/Gas 6). Place the sweet potato and oil in a bowl, and season lightly with salt and pepper. Toss together until well coated. Place on a baking tray and bake for 30 minutes, or until tender. Drain on crumpled paper towels.
2 To make the dressing, combine the curry paste, coconut milk, lime juice and sugar in a food processor.
3 Heat the oil in a small frying pan. Add the garlic and ginger and cook over low heat for 1–2 minutes, or until light brown. Remove and add to the dressing.
4 Place the sweet potato, cashews, coriander, dressing and the noodles in a large bowl and toss gently until combined. Serve immediately.

Nutrition per serve (6): Fat 29 g; Protein 12 g; Carbohydrate 46 g; Dietary fibre 6.5 g; Cholesterol 5.5 mg; 2015 kJ (480 cal)

Note: This is best assembled just before serving to prevent the noodles from becoming soggy.

SCALLOPS WITH SOBA NOODLES AND DASHI BROTH

Prep time: 10 minutes
Cooking time: 15 minutes
Serves 4

250 g soba noodles
3 tablespoons mirin
1/4 cup (60 ml) soy sauce
2 teaspoons rice wine vinegar
1 teaspoon dashi granules
2 spring onions, sliced on the diagonal
1 teaspoon finely chopped fresh ginger
24 large scallops (without roe)
5 fresh black fungus, chopped
1 sheet nori, shredded

1 Cook the noodles in a large saucepan of boiling water for 5 minutes, or until tender. Drain and rinse under cold water.
2 Place the mirin, soy sauce, rice wine vinegar, dashi granules and 3 cups (750 ml) water in a saucepan. Bring to the boil, then reduce the heat and simmer for 3–4 minutes. Add the spring onion and ginger and keep at a gentle simmer until needed.
3 Heat a chargrill or hot plate until very hot and sear the scallops on both sides, in batches, for 1 minute. Remove.
4 Divide the noodles and black fungus among four deep serving bowls. Pour 3/4 cup (185 ml) broth into each bowl and top with 6 scallops each. Garnish with the shredded nori and serve immediately.

Nutrition per serve: Fat 1 g; Protein 20 g; Carbohydrate 49 g; Dietary fibre 1.5 g; Cholesterol 25.5 mg; 1125 kJ (270 cal)

Note: If fresh black fungus is not available, use dried instead. Soak in warm water for 15–20 minutes before use.

Orange sweet potato and fried noodle salad (top) and Scallops with soba noodles and dashi broth

NOODLE TEMPURA WITH WASABI DRESSING

Prep time: 10 minutes
Cooking time: 15 minutes
Serves 4

Wasabi dressing
1/2 teaspoon wasabi paste
11/2 tablespoons Japanese
   soy sauce
3 tablespoons mirin

80 g dried ramen noodles
1 carrot, grated
2 nori sheets, shredded
2 spring onions, finely
   sliced
11/4 cups (155 g) tempura
   flour
1 cup (250 ml) iced water
oil, for deep-frying

1 To make the wasabi dressing, place the wasabi paste and a little of the soy sauce in a small bowl and combine to make a smooth paste. Add the mirin and the remaining soy sauce and stir until combined and there are no lumps. Set aside until ready to use.

2 Cook the noodles in a large saucepan of boiling salted water for 5 minutes, or until tender. Drain and rinse under running cold water. Cut the noodles into 5 cm lengths with a pair of scissors. Transfer to a large bowl.

3 Add the carrot, nori and spring onion to the noodles and combine using a wooden spoon. Refrigerate until ready.

4 Place the tempura flour in a large bowl and make a well in the centre. Pour in the iced water and stir gently with chopsticks or a fork, until the flour and water are just combined (the batter should still be a little lumpy).

5 Fill a wok or deep heavy-based saucepan one third full of oil and heat to 180°C (350°F), or until a cube of bread dropped into the oil browns in 15 seconds. Combine the noodle mixture and the tempura batter, tossing lightly. Spoon 1/4 cup (60 ml) of the noodle mixture into the oil and, using chopsticks or a fork, quickly and carefully spread the mixture out a little. Cook for 2-3 minutes, turning occasionally, or until golden brown and cooked through. Remove and drain on crumpled paper towels. Keep warm in a slow 150°C (300°F/Gas 2) oven while you repeat with the remaining mixture, to make eight patties in total. Serve with the wasabi dressing.

Nutrition per serve: Fat 13.5 g;
Protein 8 g; Carbohydrate 44 g;
Dietary fibre 4.5 g; Cholesterol
0 mg; 1370 kJ (325 cal)

Notes: When measuring out the fritter mixture, make sure you fill the cup loosely otherwise the fritters will be too dense.

Good tempura should be light and crisp and the batter should just cover the food. It should never be heavy like the traditional batter used to coat fish. The secret is to have both the food and the batter very cold. Also, avoid letting the batter stand for too long— freshly made batter will give you the best results.

Tempura is best served the moment it is ready, as the cooked batter tends to become soggy on standing.

Noodle tempura with
wasabi dressing

TIGER PRAWN AND RICE NOODLE SALAD

Prep time: 15 minutes +
  10 minutes soaking
Cooking time: 15 minutes
Serves 4

Dressing
2 tablespoons dark soy
  sauce
1 tablespoon fish sauce
2 tablespoons lime juice
1 teaspoon grated lime rind
1 teaspoon caster sugar
1 fresh red chilli, seeded
  and finely chopped
2 teaspoons finely chopped
  fresh ginger

150 g dried rice vermicelli
100 g snow peas, trimmed,
  cut in half widthways
3 tablespoons peanut oil
2/3 cup (100 g) raw
  cashews, chopped
24 raw tiger prawns, peeled,
  deveined and tails intact
1/2 cup (10 g) fresh mint,
  chopped
1/2 cup (15 g) fresh
  coriander leaves, chopped

1 To make the dressing, combine the ingredients in a small bowl.
2 Soak the noodles in boiling water for 6–7 minutes. Drain and set aside.
3 Blanch the snow peas in boiling salted water for 10 seconds. Drain and refresh in cold water.
4 Heat the oil in a wok and swirl to coat. When hot, add the cashews and stir-fry for 2–3 minutes, or until golden. Remove with a slotted spoon and drain on paper towels. Add the prawns to the wok and cook over high heat, stirring constantly, for 2–3 minutes, or until just pink. Transfer to a large bowl, pour on the dressing and toss. Chill.
5 Add the noodles, snow peas, mint, coriander and cashews, toss well and serve immediately.

Nutrition per serve: Fat 19.5 g;
Protein 32 g; Carbohydrate 32 g;
Dietary fibre 3 g; Cholesterol
170 mg; 1795 kJ (430 cal)

SPICE-CRUSTED SALMON AND NOODLE SALAD

Prep time: 15 minutes
Cooking time: 10 minutes
Serves 4

1/2 teaspoon wasabi paste
1/3 cup (80 ml) Japanese
  soy sauce
5 tablespoons mirin
1 teaspoon sugar
250 g dried somen noodles
1 teaspoon sesame oil
1 teaspoon sansho powder
1 tablespoon vegetable oil
3 salmon fillets (about 200 g
  each), skin removed
4 spring onions, finely sliced
  on the diagonal
1/2 cup (15 g) fresh
  coriander leaves
1 Lebanese cucumber,
  halved lengthways, thinly
  sliced

1 Combine the wasabi with a little of the Japanese soy sauce to form a smooth paste. Stir in the mirin, sugar and remaining soy sauce.
2 Cook the noodles in a large saucepan of boiling salted water for 2 minutes, or until tender. Drain and rinse in cold water. Transfer to a large bowl and toss with the sesame oil.
3 Combine the sansho, oil and 1/4 teaspoon salt and brush on both sides of the salmon. Heat a large frying pan over medium heat. Add the salmon and cook each side for 2–3 minutes, or until cooked to your liking. Remove from the pan and flake into large pieces with a fork.
4 Add the salmon, spring onion, coriander, cucumber and half the dressing to the noodles, then toss together. Place on a serving dish and drizzle with the remaining dressing.

Nutrition per serve: Fat 15.5 g;
Protein 38 g; Carbohydrate 46 g;
Dietary fibre 3 g; Cholesterol
78 mg; 2005 kJ (480 cal)

Tiger prawn and rice noodle salad (top), and Spice-crusted salmon and noodle salad

SOBA NOODLES WITH MISO AND BABY EGGPLANT

Prep time: 15 minutes
Cooking time: 30 minutes
Serves 4

250 g soba noodles
3 teaspoons dashi granules
1 1/2 tablespoons yellow miso
1 1/2 tablespoons Japanese soy sauce
1 1/2 tablespoons mirin
2 tablespoons vegetable oil
1/2 teaspoon sesame oil
6 baby eggplants, cut into 1 cm slices
2 cloves garlic, crushed
1 tablespoon finely chopped fresh ginger
1 cup (150 g) cooked peas
2 spring onions, sliced thinly on the diagonal
toasted sesame seeds, to garnish

1 Cook the noodles in a large saucepan of boiling water for 5 minutes. Drain and refresh with cold water.
2 Dissolve the dashi in 1 1/2 cups (375 ml) boiling water. Stir in the miso, soy and mirin.
3 Heat half the oils in a large frying pan over high heat. Cook the eggplant in two batches, for 4 minutes, or until golden on both sides. Stir in the garlic and ginger, then the miso mixture and bring to the boil. Reduce the

heat and simmer for 10 minutes, or until slightly thickened and the eggplant is cooked. Add the noodles and peas and cook for 2 minutes, or until heated through.
4 Serve in shallow bowls and garnish with spring onion and toasted sesame seeds.

Nutrition per serve: Fat 6.5 g; Protein 13 g; Carbohydrate 54 g; Dietary fibre 5.5 g; Cholesterol 0 mg; 1275 kJ (305 cal)

WARM PORK AND UDON NOODLE SALAD WITH LIME DRESSING

Prep time: 20 minutes
Cooking time: 10 minutes
Serves 4

Dressing
1/3 cup (80 ml) lime juice
1 tablespoon sesame oil
2 tablespoons ponzu
1/4 cup (90 g) honey

400 g fresh udon noodles
500 g pork fillet
1 tablespoon sesame oil
200 g roasted unsalted peanuts
2 teaspoons finely chopped fresh ginger
2 large fresh red chillies, seeded and finely diced
1 large cucumber, peeled, halved, seeds removed and julienned

200 g bean sprouts
1/2 cup (25 g) chopped fresh coriander leaves

1 Preheat the oven to moderately hot 200°C (400°F/Gas 6). To make the dressing, place the lime juice, sesame oil, ponzu and honey in a screwtop jar and shake.
2 Cook the noodles in a saucepan of boiling water for 1–2 minutes, or until tender. Drain, rinse and set aside.
3 Trim the fat and sinew off the pork and brush with the sesame oil. Season. Heat a non-stick frying pan until very hot and cook the pork for 5–6 minutes, or until browned on all sides and cooked to your liking. Remove from the pan and rest for 5 minutes.
4 Combine the noodles, peanuts, ginger, chilli, cucumber, bean sprouts and coriander and toss well. Cut the pork into thin slices, add to the salad with the dressing and toss before serving.

Nutrition per serve: Fat 36 g; Protein 48 g; Carbohydrate 53 g; Dietary fibre 7 g; Cholesterol 61.5 mg; 3020 kJ (720 cal)

Soba noodles with miso and baby eggplant (top), and Warm pork and udon noodle salad with lime dressing

PORK, PRAWN AND VERMICELLI SALAD IN LETTUCE CUPS

Prep time: 20 minutes
Cooking time: 15 minutes
Serves 6

vegetable oil, for frying
100 g dried rice vermicelli
3 tablespoons peanut oil
1 clove garlic, crushed
1 tablespoon finely chopped fresh ginger
3 spring onions, finely sliced and green ends reserved for garnish
150 g pork mince
500 g raw prawns, peeled, deveined and roughly chopped
2 tablespoons Chinese rice wine
2 tablespoons soy sauce
2 tablespoons hoisin sauce
1 tablespoon brown bean sauce
1/2 teaspoon sugar
1/4 cup (60 ml) chicken stock
12 iceburg lettuce leaves, trimmed into cups

1 Fill a deep heavy-based saucepan or deep-fryer one third full of oil and heat to 170°C (325°F), or until a cube of bread dropped into the oil browns in 20 seconds. Add the dried rice vermicelli in batches and deep-fry until puffed up but not browned—this will only take a few seconds. Remove with a slotted spoon and drain well on crumpled paper towels.
2 Heat the peanut oil in a wok over high heat and swirl to coat the side. Add the garlic, ginger and spring onion and stir-fry for 1 minute, being careful not to burn the garlic.
3 Add the pork mince to the wok, breaking up the lumps with the back of a wooden spoon, then cook for a further 4 minutes. Add the prawns and stir-fry for 2 minutes, or until they begin to change colour.
4 Add the Chinese rice wine, soy sauce, hoisin sauce, brown bean sauce, sugar, chicken stock and 1/2 teaspoon salt and stir until combined. Cook over high heat for 2 minutes, or until the mixture thickens slightly.
5 Divide the noodles among the lettuce cups, spoon the pork and prawn mixture over the noodles and garnish with the reserved spring onion. Serve at once.

Nutrition per serve: Fat 24 g; Protein 24 g; Carbohydrate 9 g; Dietary fibre 1.5 g; Cholesterol 139.5 mg; 1455 kJ (350 cal)

Notes: Make sure the pork mince is not too lean or the mixture will be dry.

Pork, prawn and vermicelli salad in lettuce cups

When deep-frying the vermicelli, take care not to allow the oil to become too hot as the noodles will expand and brown very quickly. It helps to make sure you have everything you need by your side before you start deep-frying the noodles—a slotted spoon for removing the noodles and a tray lined with crumpled paper towels.

Remember to deep-fry the noodles in small batches as they will dramatically increase in volume.

PEANUT CHICKEN NOODLE SALAD

Prep time: 30 minutes
Cooking time: 20 minutes
Serves 4

Lemon chilli dressing
2 cloves garlic, crushed
3 small fresh red chillies, seeded and finely chopped
3 tablespoons lemon juice
2 teaspoons lemon rind
1/3 cup (80 ml) fish sauce
1/2 cup (90 g) grated palm sugar
1/4 cup (60 ml) rice vinegar

350 g dried flat egg noodles
1/2 teaspoon sesame oil
1/2 teaspoon vegetable oil
1/2 cup (60 g) finely sliced spring onion
1 red capsicum, thinly sliced
1/2 cup (15 g) fresh coriander leaves
1/2 cup (10 g) fresh mint
extra oil, for pan-frying
2 eggs, lightly beaten
2 tablespoons fish sauce
2 tablespoons plain flour
2 cups (320 g) raw peanuts, ground
500 g chicken breast fillets, cut into 1 cm strips

1 Stir all the dressing ingredients in a saucepan over low heat for 2 minutes, or until the sugar dissolves. Pour into a screwtop jar and cool.
2 Cook the noodles in a large saucepan of boiling water for 3–4 minutes. Rinse and drain. Add the oils and combine to coat evenly. Toss in the spring onion, capsicum, coriander and mint.
3 Heat a little extra oil in a frying pan over medium–high heat. Combine the eggs and fish sauce in a bowl, then combine the flour and peanuts in a shallow dish. Dip each chicken strip into the egg, then the flour. Pan-fry until cooked and golden all over. Drain.
4 Shake the dressing and toss through the noodles. Place on a serving dish, topped with the chicken.

Nutrition per serve: Fat 57.5 g; Protein 34 g; Carbohydrate 99 g; Dietary fibre 11 g; Cholesterol 192 mg; 4875 kJ (1165 cal)

SEAFOOD NOODLES

Prep time: 20 minutes + 20 minutes soaking
Cooking time: 15 minutes
Serves 4

6 dried shiitake mushrooms
400 g fresh thick egg noodles
1 egg white, lightly beaten
3 teaspoons cornflour
1 teaspoon crushed sichuan peppercorns
250 g firm white fish, cut into 2 cm cubes
200 g raw prawns, peeled, deveined and tails intact
3 tablespoons peanut oil
3 spring onions, sliced on the diagonal
2 cloves garlic, crushed
1 tablespoon grated fresh ginger
225 g can bamboo shoots, thinly sliced
2 tablespoons hot chilli sauce
1 tablespoon soy sauce
2 tablespoons rice wine
3/4 cup (185 ml) fish stock

1 Soak the mushrooms in 1/2 cup (125 ml) warm water for 20 minutes. Drain. Discard the stalk, then thinly slice the caps.
2 Cook the noodles in a saucepan of boiling water for 2–3 minutes, or until just tender. Drain.
3 Blend the egg white, cornflour and half the pepper to a smooth paste. Dip the seafood into the mixture.
4 Heat 2 tablespoons of the oil in a wok. Drain the excess batter from the seafood. Stir-fry in batches over high heat until crisp and golden. Drain.
5 Clean the wok and heat the remaining oil. Toss the spring onion, garlic, ginger, bamboo shoots, mushrooms, and remaining pepper over high heat for 1 minute. Stir in the chilli and soy sauces, rice wine, stock and noodles. Add the seafood and toss until heated through.

Nutrition per serve: Fat 12.5 g; Protein 35 g; Carbohydrate 59 g; Dietary fibre 4 g; Cholesterol 124.5 mg; 2085 kJ (500 cal)

Peanut chicken noodle salad (top), and Seafood noodles

MANDARIN AND DUCK RICE PAPER ROLLS

Prep time: 40 minutes
Cooking time: Nil
Makes 24

1 whole Chinese roast duck
24 small Vietnamese rice
  paper wrappers
3 mandarins, peeled and
  segmented
1 cup (20 g) fresh mint
60 g fresh chives, cut into
  3–4 cm lengths
2 tablespoons hoisin sauce
2 tablespoons fresh
  mandarin juice

1 Remove the flesh and skin from the duck and shred into 1 cm x 3 cm pieces.
2 Working with one wrapper at a time, briefly soak each wrapper in cold water until softened, then place on a dry tea towel. Arrange 2–3 pieces of duck at the end of the wrapper closest to you. Top with 2 segments of mandarin, 3 mint leaves and several lengths of chives. Fold the end closest to you over the filling, fold in the sides and firmly roll up the rice paper to form a small spring roll.

3 Combine the hoisin sauce and mandarin juice in a bowl and serve as a dipping sauce with the rice paper rolls. These are best served immediately as the rolls will start to dry out if left for too long.

Nutrition per roll: Fat 1.4 g;
Protein 4 g; Carbohydrate 3 g;
Dietary fibre 0.5 g; Cholesterol
19.5 mg; 160 kJ (40 cal)

TAMARIND BEEF, BEAN AND HOKKIEN NOODLE STIR-FRY

Prep time: 20 minutes
Cooking time: 20 minutes
Serves 4

Tamarind sauce
1 tablespoon tamarind purée
1 tablespoon vegetable oil
1 onion, finely diced
2 tablespoons palm sugar
2 tablespoons tamari

500 g Hokkien noodles
4 beef fillet steaks (about
  120 g each)
2 tablespoons oil
3 cloves garlic, crushed
1 small fresh chilli, seeded
  and diced
300 g baby green beans,
  trimmed
100 g sugar snap peas,
  trimmed
1 tablespoon mirin
1/2 cup (15 g) finely
  chopped fresh coriander
  leaves

1 To make the sauce, dilute the tamarind in 1 cup (250 ml) hot water. Heat the oil in a saucepan. Add the onion and cook over medium heat for 6–8 minutes, or until soft and golden. Add the palm sugar and stir until dissolved. Add the tamarind liquid and tamari and simmer for 5 minutes, or until thick.
2 Rinse the noodles in a colander with warm water to soften—separate with your hands. Drain.
3 Season the steaks with salt and freshly ground black pepper. Heat half the oil in a large frying pan. Add the fillets and cook on each side for 3–4 minutes, or until cooked to your liking. Remove from the pan and rest in a warm place.
4 Heat the remaining oil in a wok and cook the garlic and chilli over high heat for 30 seconds. Add the beans and peas and cook for 2 minutes. Stir in the mirin and coriander. Add the noodles and toss until heated through.
5 Divide the noodles among four plates. Top with the steak and drizzle with the sauce.

Nutrition per serve: Fat 15.5 g;
Protein 37 g; Carbohydrate 44 g;
Dietary fibre 6 g; Cholesterol
72 mg; 1940 kJ (465 cal)

Mandarin and duck rice paper rolls (top), and Tamarind beef, bean and Hokkien noodle stir-fry

GREEN TEA NOODLE SOUP

Prep time: 10 minutes
Cooking time: 10 minutes
Serves 4

200 g dried green tea
    noodles
2 teaspoons dashi granules
1 tablespoons mirin
1 tablespoon Japanese
    soy sauce
200 g firm tofu, drained and
    cut into 1.5 cm cubes
1 sheet nori, shredded
3 teaspoons toasted
    sesame seeds

1 Cook the noodles in a large saucepan of boiling salted water for 5 minutes, or until tender. Drain and rinse under cold water.
2 Combine the dashi granules with 1.5 litres water in a large saucepan. Stir over medium–high heat until the granules are dissolved. Increase the heat to high and bring to the boil. Stir in the mirin and soy sauce.
3 Divide the noodles and tofu cubes among four serving bowls and ladle the hot stock on top. Garnish with the nori and sesame seeds. Serve immediately.

Nutrition per serve: Fat 5.5 g;
Protein 14 g; Carbohydrate 36 g;
Dietary fibre 3 g; Cholesterol
9 mg; 1045 kJ (250 cal)

TERIYAKI CHICKEN AND UDON NOODLES

Prep time: 20 minutes +
    30 minutes marinating
Cooking time: 20 minutes
Serves 4

450 g chicken breast fillets
1 clove garlic, crushed
11/2 teaspoons grated fresh
    ginger
1/3 cup (80 ml) light soy
    sauce
1 tablespoon sake
1/4 cup (60 ml) mirin
2 tablespoons peanut oil
1 teaspoon sesame oil
1 onion, cut into thin wedges
2 teaspoons sugar
6 spring onions, thinly sliced
    on the diagonal
400 g fresh udon noodles
2 teaspoons toasted black
    sesame seeds
1 tablespoon toasted
    sesame seeds

1 Trim the chicken fillets of any fat or sinew and cut into 2 cm cubes. Combine the garlic, ginger, soy sauce, sake and mirin in a large bowl. Add the chicken cubes and toss until well coated. Cover the bowl with plastic wrap and refrigerate for 30 minutes.
2 Drain the chicken and reserve the marinade. Combine the peanut and sesame oil. Heat half the oil in a wok, and when nearly smoking, stir–fry the chicken in batches until browned. Remove from the heat and keep warm. Add the remaining oil, then add the onion and stir–fry for 3–4 minutes, or until softened.
3 Meanwhile, place the reserved marinade and sugar in a small saucepan. Bring to the boil, then reduce the heat and simmer for 2 minutes, or until slightly syrupy, stirring occasionally. Remove from the heat and keep warm.
4 Return the chicken to the wok, along with the spring onion and udon noodles, tossing well to combine. Cook for 2 minutes before pouring in the reserved heated marinade. Cook for another minute.
5 Divide the noodles among four serving bowls. Sprinkle with the black and white toasted sesame seeds and serve immediately.

Nutrition per serve: Fat 13 g;
Protein 30 g; Carbohydrate 30 g;
Dietary fibre 3 g; Cholesterol
77.5 mg; 1515 kJ (360 cal)

Green tea noodle soup
(top), and Teriyaki chicken
and udon noodles

THAI BEEF SALAD RICE PAPER ROLLS

Prep time: 35 minutes +
  2 hours marinating
Cooking time: 5 minutes
Makes 16

Dipping sauce
1/4 cup (60 ml) Japanese
  soy sauce
1 tablespoon rice vinegar
1 teaspoon sesame oil
1 tablespoon mirin
2 teaspoons finely julienned
  fresh ginger

1/3 cup (80 ml) kecap manis
1/3 cup (80 ml) lime juice
1 tablespoon sesame oil
2 small fresh red chillies,
  finely chopped
300 g piece beef eye fillet
1 stem lemon grass, white
  part only, finely chopped
1/4 cup (60 ml) lime juice,
  extra
3 tablespoons finely
  chopped fresh mint
3 tablespoons finely
  chopped fresh coriander
  leaves
1 1/2 tablespoons fish sauce
16 square (16.5 cm) rice
  paper wrappers

1 To make the dipping sauce, place the Japanese soy sauce, rice vinegar, sesame oil, mirin and ginger in a small bowl and mix together well. Set aside until ready to serve.

Thai beef salad rice paper rolls

2 Mix the kecap manis, lime juice, sesame oil and half the chilli in a large bowl. Add the beef and toss well to ensure all the beef is coated. Cover with plastic wrap and refrigerate for 2 hours.
3 Heat a barbecue or chargrill plate over high heat and cook the beef for 2–3 minutes each side, or until cooked to your liking. Cool, then slice into thin strips, against the grain.
4 Combine the beef with the lemon grass, extra lime juice, mint, coriander, fish sauce and remaining chilli, then toss well.
5 Dip one rice paper wrapper at a time in warm water for a few seconds until softened. Drain, then place on a flat surface. Place a tablespoon of the mixture in the centre of the rice paper wrapper and roll up, tucking in the edges. Repeat with the remaining ingredients to make 16 rolls in total. Serve with the dipping sauce.

Nutrition per roll: Fat 1 g; Protein 4 g; Carbohydrate 3 g; Dietary fibre 0.5 g; Cholesterol 7.5 mg; 145 kJ (35 cal)

Notes: The beef should be cooked just until it is quite pink in the middle so that it remains tender.

Kecap manis is also known as sweet soy sauce. It is a thick dark sauce used in Indonesian cooking as a seasoning and condiment, particularly with satays. If it is not available, a substitute can be made—place 1 cup (250 ml) dark soy sauce, 6 tablespoons treacle and 3 tablespoons soft brown sugar in a small saucepan and simmer, stirring, until the sugar has completely dissolved.

If square rice paper wrappers are not available, use round wrappers of the same diameter and assemble them in the same way.

DEEP-FRIED CHICKEN BALLS

Prep time: 20 minutes +
  30 minutes refrigeration
Cooking time: 15 minutes
Makes about 30

50 g dried rice vermicelli
500 g chicken mince
3 cloves garlic, finely
  chopped
1 tablespoon chopped
  fresh ginger
1 fresh red chilli, seeded
  and finely chopped
1 egg, lightly beaten
2 spring onions, finely sliced
1/3 cup (20 g) chopped
  fresh coriander leaves
1/3 cup (40 g) plain flour
1/3 cup (60 g) finely
  chopped water chestnuts
oil, for deep-frying

Dipping sauce
1/2 cup (125 ml) sweet chilli
  sauce
1/2 cup (125 ml) soy sauce
1 tablespoon Chinese rice
  wine

1 Cover the vermicelli with boiling water and soak for 6–7 minutes. Drain, then cut into short lengths.
2 Combine the mince, garlic, ginger, chilli, egg, spring onion, coriander, flour and water chestnuts in a large bowl. Mix in the vermicelli and season with salt. Refrigerate for 30 minutes. Roll heaped tablespoons of mixture into balls.

3 Fill a wok or deep saucepan one third full with oil and heat to 180°C (350°F), or until a cube of bread browns in 15 seconds. Deep-fry the balls in batches for 2 minutes, or until golden brown and cooked through. Drain.
4 To make the dipping sauce, combine the sweet chilli sauce, soy sauce and rice wine. Serve with the hot chicken balls.

Nutrition per ball: Fat 6.5 g;
Protein 4 g; Carbohydrate 3.5 g;
Dietary fibre 0.5 g; Cholesterol
21 mg; 360 kJ (85 cal)

POACHED SEAFOOD BROTH WITH SOBA NOODLES

Prep time: 20 minutes
Cooking time: 20 minutes
Serves 4

250 g dried soba noodles
8 raw prawns
11/2 tablespoons finely
  chopped fresh ginger
4 spring onions, cut on
  the diagonal
100 ml light soy sauce
1/4 cup (60 ml) mirin
1 teaspoon grated palm
  sugar
300 g boneless salmon
  fillet, skinned and cut into
  5 cm strips
300 g boneless white fish
  fillet, skinned and cut into
  5 cm strips

150 g cleaned calamari
  hood, scored and cut into
  3 cm cubes
50 g mizuna, roughly
  chopped

1 Cook the noodles in a large saucepan of boiling water for 5 minutes, or until tender. Drain and rinse with cold water.
2 Peel and devein the prawns, reserving the shells and leaving the tails intact. Place the heads and shells in a large saucepan with the ginger, half the spring onion and 1.5 litres water. Bring slowly to the boil and boil for 5 minutes. Strain and discard the shells and spring onion. Return the stock to the pan. Add the soy sauce, mirin and palm sugar to the stock. Heat and stir to dissolve the sugar.
3 Add the seafood and poach over low heat for 2–3 minutes, or until just cooked. Add the remaining spring onion.
4 Divide the noodles evenly among four large bowls. Add the seafood, pour on the stock and scatter with the mizuna.

Nutrition per serve: Fat 8 g;
Protein 55 g; Carbohydrate 49 g;
Dietary fibre 1.5 g; Cholesterol
213.5 mg; 2000 kJ (480 cal)

Deep-fried chicken balls
(top), and Poached seafood
broth with soba noodles

CHICKEN, MANGO AND NOODLE SALAD WITH CHILLI DRESSING

Prep time: 15 minutes +
15 minutes soaking
Cooking time: 15 minutes
Serves 4

Dressing
3 tablespoons lime juice
1 teaspoon finely grated lime rind
2 tablespoons sweet chilli sauce
1 tablespoon fish sauce
1 tablespoon peanut oil

110 g dried rice noodle sticks
4 skinless chicken breasts
1 tablespoon peanut oil
1 medium just-ripe mango, cut into 1 cm cubes
1/2 cup (15 g) chopped fresh coriander leaves
125 g cucumber, halved lengthways and sliced
1 small red capsicum, seeded and thinly sliced
2 spring onions, thinly sliced on the diagonal

1 To make the dressing, combine all ingredients.
2 Cover the noodles with hot water and soak for 15 minutes. Drain. Transfer to a large bowl.
3 Toss the chicken with the oil and season lightly.

Chicken, mango and noodle salad with chilli dressing (top), and Eggplant and buckwheat noodle salad

Chargrill or grill for 6–8 minutes on each side. Rest for 5 minutes, and slice on the diagonal.
4 Toss together the chicken, mango, coriander, cucumber, capsicum, spring onion, noodles and dressing.

Nutrition per serve: Fat 10.5 g;
Protein 29 g; Carbohydrate 29 g;
Dietary fibre 2.5 g; Cholesterol
83 mg; 1355 kJ (325 cal)

EGGPLANT AND BUCKWHEAT NOODLE SALAD

Prep time: 15 minutes +
10 minutes soaking
Cooking time: 15 minutes
Serves 4–6

10 g dried shiitake mushrooms
350 g buckwheat (soba) noodles
2 teaspoons sesame oil
3 tablespoons tahini
1 tablespoon light soy sauce
1 tablespoon dark soy sauce
1 tablespoon honey
2 tablespoons lemon juice
3 tablespoons peanut oil
2 Japanese eggplants, cut into very thin strips
2 carrots, julienned
10 spring onions, cut on the diagonal
6 fresh shiitake mushrooms, thinly sliced
1 cup (50 g) roughly chopped fresh coriander leaves

1 Soak the dried shiitake mushrooms in 1/2 cup (125 ml) hot water for 10 minutes. Drain, reserving the liquid. Discard the woody stems and finely slice the caps.
2 Cook the noodles in a saucepan of boiling water for 5 minutes, or until tender. Drain. Refresh under cold water then toss with 1 teaspoon of the sesame oil.
3 Combine the tahini, light and dark soy sauce, honey, lemon juice, 2 tablespoons of the reserved mushroom liquid and the remaining sesame oil in a food processor until smooth.
4 Heat 2 tablespoons of the peanut oil over high heat. Add the eggplant and cook, turning often, for 4–5 minutes, or until soft and golden. Drain on paper towels.
5 Heat the remaining oil. Add the carrot, spring onion and fresh and dried mushrooms. Cook, stirring constantly, for 1–2 minutes, or until just softened. Remove from the heat and toss with the noodles, eggplant and dressing. Garnish with the coriander.

Nutrition per serve (6): Fat 14 g;
Protein 13 g; Carbohydrate 52 g;
Dietary fibre 4 g; Cholesterol
0 mg; 1540 kJ (370 cal)

LAMB AND RICE NOODLE SALAD WITH PEANUT DRESSING

Prep time: 25 minutes +
1 hour marinating
Cooking time: 5 minutes
Serves 4

500 g lamb fillet, cut
lengthways into thin strips
2 tablespoons light soy sauce
1 tablespoon rice wine
125g dried rice noodle sticks
1 telegraph cucumber,
unpeeled, cut into long
thin strips with a
vegetable peeler
100 g chopped unsalted
toasted peanuts
fresh coriander sprigs,
to garnish

Spicy peanut dressing
3 cloves garlic
175 g smooth peanut butter
4 tablespoons soy sauce
1 cup (30 g) fresh coriander
leaves
1 tablespoon rice wine
vinegar
1 tablespoon Chinese rice
wine or dry sherry
2 tablespoons palm sugar
1 small fresh red chilli,
roughly chopped

1 Combine the lamb, soy sauce and rice wine in a bowl. Cover and marinate for 1 hour.
2 To make the spicy peanut dressing, purée all the ingredients and 2 tablespoons water in a blender until smooth.
3 Soak the noodles in a bowl of boiling water for 15 minutes. Drain, then rinse under cold water.
4 Heat a chargrill or grill until very hot and sear the lamb slices in batches for 30 seconds on each side, or until cooked to your liking, then transfer to a large bowl. Add the noodles, cucumber and 3/4 of the dressing and toss to combine. Serve on a dish and drizzle with the remaining dressing. Scatter with the peanuts and garnish with the coriander sprigs.

Nutrition per serve: Fat 39 g;
Protein 50 g; Carbohydrate 36 g;
Dietary fibre 8.5 g; Cholesterol
82.5 mg; 2940 kJ (700 cal)

PORK AND BROWN BEAN NOODLES

Prep time: 10 minutes
Cooking time: 15 minutes
Serves 4–6

3 tablespoons brown bean
sauce
2 tablespoons hoisin sauce
3/4 cup (180 ml) chicken
stock
1/2 teaspoon sugar
2 tablespoons peanut oil
3 cloves garlic, finely
chopped
6 spring onions, sliced, white
and green parts separated
650 g pork mince
500 g fresh Shanghai
noodles
1 telegraph cucumber,
halved lengthways, seeded
and sliced on the diagonal
1 cup (30 g) fresh coriander
leaves
1 cup (90 g) bean sprouts
1 tablespoon lime juice

1 Combine the bean and hoisin sauces, stock and sugar until smooth.
2 Heat the oil in a wok or large frying pan. Add the garlic and spring onion (white part) and cook for 10–20 seconds. Add the pork and cook over high heat for 2–3 minutes, or until it has changed colour. Add the bean mixture, reduce the heat and simmer for 7–8 minutes.
3 Cook the noodles in a large saucepan of boiling water for 4–5 minutes, or until tender. Drain and rinse, then divide among serving bowls. Toss together the cucumber, coriander, bean sprouts, lime juice and remaining spring onion (green part). Spoon the brown sauce over the noodles and top with the cucumber mixture.

Nutrition per serve (6): Fat 14 g;
Protein 32 g; Carbohydrate 50 g;
Dietary fibre 4 g; Cholesterol
76.5 mg; 1905 kJ (455 cal)

Lamb and rice noodle salad
with peanut dressing (top),
and Pork and brown
bean noodles

RARE BEEF FILLET WITH CELLOPHANE NOODLES AND GINGER DRESSING

Prep time: 15 minutes +
    5 minutes soaking
Cooking time: 10 minutes
Serves 4

400 g top-grade beef fillet
2 tablespoons peanut oil
250 g cellophane noodles
1/2 teaspoon sesame oil
2 spring onions, thinly sliced
    on the diagonal

Ginger dressing
11/2 tablespoons finely
    chopped fresh ginger
3 tablespoons light soy
    sauce
3 tablespoons mirin
1 teaspoon sugar
2 teaspoons rice wine
    vinegar

1 Trim the beef fillet of any excess fat or sinew, then sprinkle with freshly ground black pepper. Heat the peanut oil in a large frying pan. When very hot, sear the meat in batches on all sides for 3 minutes, or until brown. The meat needs to remain very pink on the inside. Remove from the frying pan and allow to cool. Cover and refrigerate until completely cold.

2 Place the noodles in a heatproof bowl, cover with boiling water and soak for 3–4 minutes. Drain and rinse under cold water. Return the noodles to the bowl, add the sesame oil and toss well together.

3 To make the ginger dressing, combine the chopped ginger in a small bowl with the light soy sauce, mirin, sugar and rice wine vinegar, stirring until the sugar has completely dissolved. Set aside until ready to use.

4 Add half the spring onion to the bowl of noodles, toss together well, then place on a large serving platter. Cut the beef into thin slices, then arrange in a mound on top of the noodles.

5 Warm the dressing slightly over low heat, then pour over the beef and noodles. Scatter with the remaining spring onion and serve immediately.

Nutrition per serve: Fat 10.5 g; Protein 23 g; Carbohydrate 56 g; Dietary fibre 0.5 g; Cholesterol 60 mg; 1730 kJ (415 cal)

Notes: This dish is served cold and can be prepared a couple of hours ahead or even the day before serving, then assembled at the last minute.

Variation: For a delicious alternative, try making this dish with salmon instead of beef. Remove the skin from 400 g salmon and season well on both sides. Heat the peanut oil in a large frying pan and cook the fish on both sides for 2–3 minutes, or until cooked to your liking. The salmon should be cooked, but still quite pink on the inside. Remove from the frying pan and allow to cool a little. Using your fingers, gently flake the salmon into large bite-sized pieces, arrange on top of the noodles and pour on the dressing.

This noodle dish makes a lovely summer lunch idea.

Rare beef fillet with cellophane noodles and ginger dressing

PHAD THAI CAKES

Prep time: 15 minutes +
  15 minutes soaking
Cooking time: 40 minutes
Makes 6

50 g rice noodle sticks
1 tablespoon peanut oil
3 chicken thigh fillets,
  trimmed
9 eggs, lightly beaten
2 tablespoons fish sauce
1 tablespoon palm sugar
1 tablespoon lime juice
12 cooked prawns, peeled
  and finely chopped
1/3 cup (20 g) chopped
  fresh coriander leaves

1 Preheat the oven
to moderate 180°C
(350°F/Gas 4). Grease
six Texas muffin holes.
2 Soak the noodles in
boiling water for
15 minutes. Drain and
set aside.
3 Heat the oil in a frying
pan. Season the chicken,
then cook over high
heat for 4–5 minutes on
each side, or until just
cooked. Remove and
when cool enough, slice
thinly. Combine the
eggs, fish sauce, palm
sugar and lime juice in
a bowl.
4 Divide the noodles
among the muffin holes,
pushing up the side.
Place the chicken and
prawns on the noodles
and sprinkle with
coriander. Fill each hole
with the egg mixture.

Bake for 25–30 minutes,
or until cooked. Serve
warm or at room
temperature.

Nutrition per cake: Fat 18 g;
Protein 39 g; Carbohydrate 8 g;
Dietary fibre 0.5 g; Cholesterol
422 mg; 1450 kJ (345 cal)

GREEN TEA NOODLE SALAD WITH LAMB, CUCUMBER AND TOMATO

Prep time: 20 minutes +
  2 hours marinating
Cooking time: 10 minutes
Serves 4

1 tablespoon vegetable oil
1 teaspoon hot mustard
2 tablespoons balsamic
  vinegar
400 g lamb fillet
250 g green tea noodles
2 tablespoons soy sauce
1/2 teaspoon sugar
1 tablespoon mirin
1 teaspoon sesame oil
2 Lebanese cucumbers, cut
  in half lengthways and
  thinly sliced on the diagonal
2 large tomatoes, cut into
  1 cm cubes
1/2 cup (15 g) fresh
  coriander leaves
2 spring onions, thinly sliced
  on the diagonal
1 tablespoon sesame
  seeds, lightly toasted

1 Combine the oil,
mustard, 1 tablespoon
balsamic vinegar and

1/2 teaspoon pepper in a
bowl. Add the lamb and
toss well to coat. Cover
with plastic wrap and
refrigerate for 2 hours.
2 Cook the noodles in
a saucepan of boiling
water for 5 minutes,
or until tender. Rinse
thoroughly under cold
water and drain well.
Combine the soy sauce,
sugar, mirin, sesame
oil, the remaining
balsamic vinegar and
1/2 teaspoon salt and stir
until the sugar dissolves.
Add the noodles and
toss to coat.
3 Place the cucumber,
tomato and 1/2 teaspoon
salt in a bowl and toss
well. Add the noodles,
coriander and spring
onion and toss together.
4 Cook the lamb fillet
on a very hot chargrill
for 4–5 minutes, or until
browned on all sides and
cooked to your liking.
Remove from the heat
and rest for 10 minutes.
Divide the noodle
mixture among serving
plates. Slice the lamb
thinly and arrange on
top. Sprinkle with the
sesame seeds and serve.

Nutrition per serve: Fat 13 g;
Protein 31 g; Carbohydrate 37 g;
Dietary fibre 3.5 g; Cholesterol
74 mg; 1635 kJ (390 cal)

Phad Thai cakes (top), and
Green tea noodle salad
with lamb, cucumber
and tomato

STIR-FRIED LAMB WITH MINT, CHILLI AND SHANGHAI NOODLES

Prep time: 15 minutes
Cooking time: 15 minutes
Serves 4–6

400 g Shanghai noodles
1 teaspoon sesame oil
2 tablespoons peanut oil
220 g lamb fillet, cut into
    thin strips
2 cloves garlic, crushed
2 fresh red chillies, seeded
    and finely sliced
1 tablespoon oyster sauce
2 teaspoons palm sugar
2 tablespoons fish sauce
2 tablespoons lime juice
1/2 cup (10 g) fresh mint,
    chopped
lime wedges, to garnish

1 Cook the noodles in a large saucepan of boiling water for 4–5 minutes. Drain, then rinse in cold water. Add the sesame oil and toss through.
2 Heat the peanut oil in a wok or large frying pan over high heat. Add the lamb and cook in batches for 1–2 minutes, or until just browned. Return all the meat to the pan and add the garlic and chilli. Cook for 30 seconds then add the oyster sauce, palm

Stir-fried lamb with mint, chilli and Shanghai noodles (top), and Sticky pork with egg noodles

sugar, fish sauce, lime juice and noodles. Cook for another 2–3 minutes, or until the noodles are warm. Stir in the mint and serve immediately with the lime wedges.

Nutrition per serve (6): Fat 7.5 g; Protein 15 g; Carbohydrate 37 g; Dietary fibre 2 g; Cholesterol 33 mg; 1170 kJ (280 cal)

STICKY PORK WITH EGG NOODLES

Prep time: 20 minutes
Cooking time: 40 minutes
Serves 4

100 ml dark soy sauce
2 tablespoons hoisin sauce
2 tablespoons honey
2 teaspoons soft brown
    sugar
750 g meaty pork belly
    (off the bone, rind on),
    cut into 8 x 2 cm strips
150 g snake beans, cut into
    2 cm lengths
375 g fresh thin egg noodles
1 tablespoon peanut oil
2 cloves garlic, crushed
1 tablespoon finely chopped
    fresh ginger
250 g baby bok choy,
    quartered
2 tablespoons soy sauce
1 teaspoon sesame oil
1 tablespoon sesame seeds

1 Preheat the oven to moderately hot 200°C (400°F/Gas 6). Combine the soy and hoisin sauces, honey and brown sugar

in a small bowl. Place the pork strips side by side in a baking dish and pour on the honey soy mixture. Bake for 30 minutes, turning the slices half-way through cooking. Remove from the oven.
2 Meanwhile, blanch the beans in a saucepan of boiling salted water for 15 seconds. Remove with a slotted spoon and refresh in cold water. Bring the water back to the boil and cook the noodles for 1 minute. Drain and rinse under cold water. Set aside.
3 Heat a large frying pan. Add the pork and 1 cup (250 ml) of the marinade and cook over high heat for 2 minutes on each side, or until the sauce thickens. Remove and cool slightly.
4 Heat the peanut oil in a wok, add the garlic and ginger and cook over high heat for 30 seconds. Add the baby bok choy and cook, stirring, for 3–4 minutes, or until tender. Add the noodles, beans, soy sauce, sesame oil and seeds. Simmer for 2 minutes. Divide among four bowls, placing the syrupy pork pieces on the top.

Nutrition per serve: Fat 49.5 g; Protein 62 g; Carbohydrate 69 g; Dietary fibre 5.5 g; Cholesterol 179 mg; 4045 kJ (965 cal)

Index